Bruises,
Birthmarks
& Other Calamities

Bruises, Birthmarks & Other Calamities
©Nadine Klassen and Cathexis Northwest Press

No part of this book may be reproduced without written permission of the publisher or author, except in reviews and articles.

First Printing: 2021

Paperback ISBN: 978-1-952869-42-6
Cover art by C. M. Tollefson
Designed and edited by C. M. Tollefson

Cathexis Northwest Press

cathexisnorthwestpress.com

Bruises, Birthmarks & Other Calamities

Poems by Nadine Klassen

Cathexis Northwest Press

Medical Emergency	13
Editing a Poem about My Mother	14
My Father's Grief at the Kitchen Table	16
Him as Ariel	17
Hang on, Dear Life	19
Seasons at the Point of no Return	21
The Silver Bowl	22
Why I Hate March	23
A Human Could Swim Through a Whale's Veins	24
An Asylum of Jaws	26
Things I Wish My Mother Told Me I now Tell Myself in the Mirror	27
To the Pigeons in the Underground Car Park	28
MaleV(i)olence	30
Rapture of the Deep	32
The Night around My Neck is Waiting	33
Your End of The Body	35
Achilles Heel	36
Aglow in Mucosa	37
When I Come Home I Won't Be A Lover	38
Thread and Tyre	40

Medical Emergency

You amputate
one door from the other,
the black bag
of your arms, heavy with their fire-
proof bones. Used air seeps
through the injury.
Your thoughts are as follows:
                      Submit
a different
name. More
blood-
waste.   But here, the body wants to remain its own relic.
                              You scratch your father's voice
                              into the gullible white above a line.

How even the sharp eye-
ball of the pen rolling
back
into its own socket and out again
with its blue blood   looks almost like hope.
                              It can catch light
and dry it.
As if pale, empty
nipples; even the skin
under a layer of hair doesn't
want to nurse the electrodes   into believing
                              you are alive. You want to be
                              rhythm, printed
flat, a needle that fell
into the stack
of linoleum grey. For no machine
to pin-point   pulse.

The nurse rips
your heart out   by its tongue. You see the way it exhumes
                              language, peak for peak.

You take its beating-
graph

                              like a newborn's
                              cry.

Editing a Poem about My Mother

Garamond, size twelve.
Kill all the darlings;

I usually don't get attached to anything
that has to do with my mother.

Circle the part that likens her to a pair of scissors,
the part where she cuts my head off, just standing.

Write "flower" instead, write "rose",
 these poems are much too heavy

for the neck of a tulip.
I rewrite the line where I hyperbole

her into a million times of absence.
Write how she made me soup

those times I was sick.
How she kept an eye

on my weight
when it went wandering

to a smaller size of jeans.
Personify her Giving Hands,

personify her Nurturing,
personify her Humour;

our laughter a run-on-sentence.
I underline a thought grudge-red,

where she says I'm "normal"
because I don't weave daisies

into another woman's hair
and crown her with all the love-me's

- crown her girlfriend.
Girlfriend used to be a cuss

word on my mother's tongue
you'd never hear her say out loud.

Lengthen that sentence to the width of the acceptance
I find in her now. The stanza about her praying for my soul

before dinner stays.
I cut out the line where my mother's tongue

is a foreign language;
a past-tense built out of silence.

Instead, I write that we talk on the phone now,
more often than we used to.

I count all the good-bi's in the poem:
"**bilingual**", "**bisexual**", "**bipolar**".

Let them stand bold like **my mother**,
birthing me more than once.

Add punctuation. Add an exclamation mark
after a metaphor in which I am a question

she is the answer to!
Italic her as *shoulder*,

italic her as *apology*,
italic her asking *what's it like* being me.

Skip an entire stanza where she gave
the leaflet about the information evening on mental health

for relatives and spouses away to someone else.
I plural her forgiveness into an eraser

for the lines I've spent making her the
villain. I give the poem a title that gives

me closure. Change
the format to couplets

to make it a love poem. Weave out
all the love-me-nots I have ever handed her.

All I want to do now,
is write her love poems.

My Father's Grief at the Kitchen Table
After Warsan Shire

Another day stands
on a three-legged stool.
Or, my father's laugh lines

flatten to a black tie.
He's been practicing crying
over onions.

I, a layered globe, peel
my multitudes as if for him to eat.
Papa, death came on its running feet

I was dead before
I knew I was dying.
It has always been this way

or another;
I foster a repetition of funerals
beneath my veneer.

Here, the cutting board
of my tongue is my open casket.
Papa, I'll tell you what you need

to know.
But there are things a world cannot hold -
my father's grief at the kitchen table.

The probability of language
lowers into the grave in weeps.
The day is such a clumsy thing.

Have I told you,
there was never a knife in his hand.

Him as Ariel

& one day, you will become a son.
A golden boy, two legs, ten toes, prance
& prance and forget

                about the water. Your groin
                will wilt to vinegar.
                You will be a coward, still

& so fully, but at least
your stepmother

will love you
like her own.

My my,
where will you go then,
with all that you've done?

Who will you touch but yourself?

You will be a son,
but for now, you milk

the indifference
from her hands, merboy.
           Force what she couldn't give

                you out of women with their legs
                as fins. O, how you bathed
                in my pores & what a trembling
                to extend skin like this.

The clouds have balmed
all that they could, but my body
still remembers how you ruled it

missing. My identity questions me
& survival sings its synonyms.

I have replaced my bones
with clock hands, but I am still
something to be dismantled.

One day, you will dry your feet
& call her *mother*

& she will call you *good.*
You will look in the mirror

& cry & call it
retrospective.
You will walk

away from this with silver linings
around your body. Even your father
will swear on you.

Hang on, Dear Life
An Ode to the Absence of Mania and Depression

You have been tedious.
Same old, same new. The only change

are toothbrush-heads
and weeks. But I like

listening to you repeat yourself
religiously; morning, afternoon,

another dull evening.
Routine, like a prayer before bed

for war to end or better
weather on a birthday.

Like my father, on about the paint
job on the house or, about my mother's

way of planting hydrangeas too close
to the hedge. Like my mother's

hands, so quick to dig out copper
pennies when she sees them on sale.

I have taken up weaving
and embroidery so I can teach my fingers

how to feed their need for reassurance
and run the same road twice.

Life, I can count on you to bring
me the bliss of recurrence. Direction drizzles

through me like music must, through
a mirror. Another evening song, like callous

on my feet. I know you were made
for more. But when I play the piano

and sing what's not in the charts
anymore on the local

radio station, I keep my foot heavy on the pedal;
even in music I search for monotony.

I start each day born new,
recycled sun, a paper bag.

A tulip growing against
its cut - in the drought

of wild vases
I have nothing

to make sense of, and the predictability
of its lifespan gives

my grief an early start. What it is to be
foreseeable and not become a future.

My time has been many times,
but I have a back to turn

on every hand of the clock
that has ever pointed toward me.

So hang on, dear life, while I find myself
in an absence that doesn't leave a hole.

Seasons at the Point of no Return

Because grief came

    un-ribboned and I cried

by the door like a pine.

    I wore that autumn

dress with the copper

    flowers

and shed each one

    doorwards, awaywards,

runwards. Until

    I was naked with just myself

to blame. September

    knelt into its last breath,

so eager

    to earn a new name.

I walked around

    still answering to Season.

I worked, paid my rent

    on time, dreamt of a new life

in New Zealand.

    I beaded

the letters

    you never wrote me

around my neck.

    Remembered your birthday

and the way your finger

    flips up like a meerkat

when you scroll past me on your

    phone. Before you answer,

let me ask:

    did I chase you

to another?

    Doorwards, awaywards,

runawaywards.

    I couldn't hold you, love.

Love, you've made me

    a fool. Season,

and yet, I cannot return

    to you.

The Silver Bowl

I held him,
my hands, a cross-stitch
over the cloth on his slouched
back. My knuckles, ten little beads,
when I felt it: the carrying
his shoulders have had to do.
The weight of wet soil
thrown into the grave of his will.
A man in a hospital bed, I wish
he'd never have had to endure
the coming of this in ours;
his sheets then, wefts of pain and me
not noticing as we lay next
to each other. His gown now, embroidered
with my arms and all the cables
they could find. I took a bowl, silver
as a needle, from the medical cart
and filled it with water.
Then, I washed his bruised back and
shoulders, his long legs. There was
nothing else that I could have done,
but to keep my thread-arms moving
across his skin. To mend what was there.

Why I Hate March
After Natalie Diaz

In March,
the trees spill all of their secrets, everyone
betrays the moon; I'm sick of the sight

of him. The snow threatens dog owners
with the exact kidney function of their
dogs. I've never seen cars as exhausted.

In town, the streets are empty as a bed
of nails, no one wants the feeling of drowning
open mouthed feet under a rug of mudded

snow. What I mean to say is,
that this has always been
just as much torture

for me, with winter on the rack of March.
That once, when I was pulled apart,
some woman in me asked for a hangman

- a guillotine. Sudden silver.
That I wanted
for it all to end. So I dialed a friend's number,
texted another one, saw my mother and father.

This is the way
I had given up every name
I loved; I was sure, I was alone.

I showered and shaved, dressed
my stretched out body in lounge wear.
Ate for the last time before

I lay in my own bathtub -
hands, popped the blisters
like knuckles, floated in white ice cubes,

knowing what a selfish kind
of brutal it would be to make
my lover's lap my deathbed.

Now, every time March pulls out its pliers
and knives, my last meal drips
onto my scalp - the light stays on all night.

A Human Could Swim Through a Whale's Veins
After Noah Baldino, After Meghann Plunkett

I enter the doctor's office with ear-warmer-seashells.
I miss the sound of the ocean of my own blood, I tell him.
He directs me to a plasma-yellow chair by the foot of his desk.

*I've never been a good swimmer either, I'm easily
exhausted, and I worry that I will be an embolism,
again.* A clotted body, fetal position - another round

of depression. I heard somewhere that most lung
embolisms are diagnosed after death. I ask my doctor if this
is true, he doesn't say or do anything with his head. I think of all

the trains and rooftops and rivers that became a diagnosis,
treated only with a grave. I think of all the suicides that were
in me. Of how lucky I am. I tell him, *I'm not in a killing*

kinda mood today. He gets out his bible and says
something about Jonah and stomachs and do I feel
that way. But *I say, this time I'm not so much being digested.*

Less like shit. It's more lively than that, more of a rush.
He prescribes me a knife and says, *you gotta kill
something to feel nothing*. I wiggle around in my chair,

nibble on the ring around my finger and say, *I tried killing myself
with oxytocin last night*, which is just another way of saying I hugged

the pill bottle to fall asleep. I can be honest with him
that way; he knows my ups and downs - my mixed phases.

- one time, I fantasized with so much care
about what it would be like
to die drowning.
                    The next day I
            went to the animal shelter to
        adopt a Husky. I didn't go through with either.

He looks at how my legs are still tangled up in each other, double-
crossed; nothing fits between a neck and a noose. Nothing fits between
my legs. He reaches for his Nicholas Sparks books and reads something

about being a bird if someone else is also a bird
and do I feel that way. I say, *sure* and *I just wanted to fly
the fuck away*. I didn't like the other bird. *He never asked me what I wanted*, I say.

He calls a nurse. When she walks in, I notice she's dressed in new
years' red for good luck. They chant the blood test song and she rings
the needle. A ritual only bipolar patients get to be part of.

Routine is important for us. She draws
a madness of firecracker-blood, sparks
my fireworks onto a pregnancy test, while I wonder if I will

carry this illness to full term. I'm scared of the thought
of the labour. Still positive, but in the little graph,
the pillars of trauma spiked.

He asks, *is that why your legs are holding each other?*
I say, *sure.*

An Asylum of Jaws

Mom, we're way past delivery room enquiries,
but I need you
to double-check my fingers;
my hands are lost
in count. And this is as physical
                          as it isn't;
sometimes my body is an asylum of jaws,
clenched so tight, I have to wear
a mouthguard.
                Sometimes *it's all in my head.*
10, 11, 12,
I don't mean to
symptomify everything,
           but do you see it, this enduring of my own body?
           I boil with the kettle.
           I weep with the doors.
           I am teething neon lights.
           You ask if this is just hormonal.
I wear trauma-sized T-shirts
which is arbitrary -
           sometimes a crop top
will do.
     It's not that I blame you,
     Mom, it's just a coping mechanism.
I know you're concerned about my kidneys
and liver.
           You don't mind the pills
           for the migraines so much.
But I like my Abilify-ability to drown
the hair dryer noise in a bathtub
of my symptoms,
           may they rest in peace.

Things I Wish My Mother Told Me I now Tell Myself in the Mirror

I'm sorry.
You are a good woman. It was never your fault - so your skin is a windchime behind a window, so your skin is music pulled from its pulse. It's okay, when you became a bird I couldn't help but be song. It's okay, my moonbell daughter, ring your night's arrival and I will answer the door of day. Stay late, in your dressing gown, unshowered and unshaven. It's okay, I've always loved you like a miracle its maker; my being speaks of your existence. You are a rebellion of beautiful things. O, sweet twilight, young peach. You hold your pit so tight with all that blush. Loosen up a little. Don't be afraid of your laugh lines telling the jokes. You tired sun, yawning without a hand on your mouth. Look at the birds fly in the mirror. You tickle on the feet of sky, when the day gets too heavy. Who's gonna teach you about love? Who's gonna withhold all the heartbreak? O, you sudden thing, I can't take my eyes off you. I am sorry I sometimes looked at you in abbreviations. I am sorry I fed you question marks. O, you hungry thing. It's okay to be hungry. You tender violence, you survival. You freckled shore, siren. O, you, you don't have stay when love has left. Capital Y You, tree of answer. You fraction of Yourself - still becoming. It's okay, You exist despite Your beliefs. It's okay to learn to forgive the endings. It's okay, loneliness can be a lesson, too. It was never Your fault. You are a good woman.
I'm sorry.

To the Pigeons in the Underground Car Park
After Hanif Abdurraqib

I understand how a sky can be overwhelming.
How you might need some time to check the oil

on your feathers, again. Need to empty
that trash can, need a proper wing-

man. Some time to fiddle
with your coo in the ignition of small talk.

A moment to be inspired by the fumes
of someone else's arrival. You still give a shit

on how they got there. Let me tell you, I've practiced
coming here just to have somewhere to go.

To learn the echo of a slammed door
like I wish I could the consequence

of a decision,
just before I make one. I, too, worry

about the cat in the tree.
I know it can't be easy to carry

that wingbeat, knowing it could cause
a storm. How you had to dodge

the blue of directions and still want
what you can't have; the tears

of an ex-lover,
a windowsill without nails. Still fly

into windows with bird-
stickers on them; lonely find the lonely.

See, even we have learned to live
in the sky. And when I say your kind,

I mean myself mostly, has snapped
its neck on the mirror

of a window. I'm only saying that I saw
a version of myself in a busy window

and didn't have the patience
to get to know her. Maybe

I was scared she would find me
boring. There is a reason we laugh

in the basement.
So close to the gutter, I am sorry

to bring up the name of another species
when I am talking about you.

But you are growing fur-
ther away from your own. I, too, have found

most of my decisions to be rudimentary.
Otherwise, they are more femur;

only stretching things out that will bend
eventually. I, too, claim my feeding place

where others leave breadcrumbs.
This counter-evolution fits me

like a seatbelt-
clip its orange mouth. My dear,

my kind, myself included, calls you rat
of the sky. And the gift of purpose

in such a crowd can be rare. I don't know
what to call myself now,

that I don't have anything
to deliver.

MaleV(i)olence

I will bless the day
you touch yourself,
pull your groin

up towards hell, climax
yourself into existence
& it burns slaughter-

glow onto your stomach.
I bless the day you look
almost palpable in sunlight

& so night, always night.
You will be marked
lust, damned & bodiless.

You've made enough
mirrors out of skin,
only for the heartbeat.

When your mother bathes
you, she will bathe you in hot coals

& call you Son of Hell.

She will not teach you
how to love
yourself.

She will see your skin
undressed, all sex & possession.

She will make your bed
with the moment it was over,

beg the devil for forgiveness.

She will see how you blur
into a beginning, how some things
consist only of preparation

& aftercare, like suicides & love
notes. She will take you to the river's mouth,
where the water mourns its choices

& say *regret, regret, regret.*

But you haven't found anyone
deep enough for that, yet.
& so pain, but only someone else's.

I bless the day your mother shears

your shoulder blades with nail
clippers. I bless the day your mother
won't forgive you. She won't forgive you.

Rapture of the Deep

That night you set
        down against the wall like a stone
into a gutted ocean.
        I worried you would not take
the tiled ground for what it was, chip it open
        like another bottle
of beer. What does your mother look like
        underwater - does her body
language become liquid, is she almost unhinged?
        A jaw unhooked from its frame,
like fish from their skeleton, useless
        for keeping secrets
like bodies? Is her voice a depth
        to leave you
thirsty? A violin played
        to a childhood room, until both their bones
quiver. Does it still sound like the love
        she hid in the top drawer,
only like expensive
        lingerie? Is it still only something to bathe
her lovers in? Here you are,
        already thinking slow, sedated. Her grey hair
smells like the smoke
        of your cigarette. Now driftwood, a hollow
anchor. Sinking or rising, depending
        on which way is up in the first place.
Your face is wet
        with hers, like she had been heaved
through your eyes. She hasn't died yet,
        but you've lost
your judgement, so who's to say.
        You've given her a sea-burial everytime
you drank. Left her eyes
        uncoined, her voyage an open
end. You forgot
        you're not the one supposed
to drown.

The Night around My Neck is Waiting

On your chest, the water
lilies are drowning

in the rain of my mouth.
Ponds, a shy pink

under a sky, all heron,
waiting for fish

to blister up.
My hands, so ripe they spit

out their knuckles
like hearts. Breathe against

my breath, we burn
our own small storm

under this ceiling.
I kiss you

with a silent thunder
tongue. I kiss you silver

light and light,
again, glove my body

in your breath, again. We know
about skies that forget

their bruises; we've seen
the commercials

for wipes that clean
off fingerpaint. You lick

off every setting sun
on my body, Icarus.

Fall into a bite,
the night around my neck

is waiting.
I empty my teeth

at the shrine
of your shoulders. You are all

I have to offer. I trace
the brass frontiers

of your sweet-talker
skin. Bend to your soft

leather tongue. I think
my mother will touch
me soon and I will

still smell of lust.
The suns on my chest
still risen - a full day

climbing the ladder
of my ribs.
I will be so clean

of bruises, she won't
remember me.

Your End of The Body

We lie at barren breasts. If it rained
on your end of the body I wouldn't know
about it. Love is a mammal, too. A blue

whale, or its calf. This is the circle of life:
we come to it and it comes to us. Both,
kids out on the field

of the universe, learning to walk
in the gravity of our secrets. Love tells,
it always does, with its wonky knees.

But what do I know - I don't listen. Time passes,
gentle as a bruise, and with no room left
on our skin is passing still. It's just that neither

one of us counting anymore.
I was never convinced
by the idea of best friends, anyway.

Not until you told me that we were.
How I wish we could

love each other again. I'd pray
to the universe, I'd give it space.

I should be thankful,
I have loved you,

fully. I will cheers to the birthmarks
we've made look like bruises,

I'll cheers to the bruises, birthmarks,
and other calamities; trauma

on our earlobe, depression on our right
hip. But I feel our bodies now,

laboured exhausted, our breasts
empty pearls
of milk.

Achilles Heel

We listened to *Candyshop*
       with our minds as messy
as teenage rooms, riddled with

lollipop wrapping paper. Our unmade
       beds, plates of orange
slices became boys to practice kissing

in Hershey Chocolate dreams.
       Our ripening bodies, breasts
budding in wonderbras,

or hidden with the other
       monsters under the bed
of a fine rib sports bra. I remember

the maiden name of my first boyfriend's mother
       and the bra I wore
when I learned it:

Chocolate flowers with cream-
       lace, underwire
B-cup. Puberty held me

by my heart when it dipped
       me in the teenage
laundry pile of experience.

The sugar rush
       of being woundable.
The boys I kissed, their mothers,

who didn't know
       my name. There was so much
promise when there was none.

Aglow in Mucosa

We haven't returned
each other's bodies to grief.

With both of us
under white sheets, the ghosting became
redundant, so for a while after it was over,

we hid ourselves under the same.
Skipped the round edges of our fingers
across the water of our skin, knowing

about things that drown. A stone, love:
just to hold what you remember.
But I don't have the truth

of your skin anymore,
and middle of sun-wilt,
most other bodies are a bother.

//

I press my lipstick-mouth
to a folded sheet of toilet paper.
It holds on like a lover

you don't want to stick around
for breakfast. Pink like stolen
lighters, cigarette smoke

in front of red neons.
A continent aglow in mucosa;
this is the heart of the world

I am holding in my mouth
and cannot get to spin:

I want you to stay.

When I Come Home I Won't Be A Lover
for my love

                  I.

My hair will oil
its split ends. The barrel
core will speak its heart

& I will ignore it. I won't know
where to fire mine. I will strip
the rain from its water until

        it is only thirst.
I will strip my skin from its flesh until
        it is only muscle memory.

I will paint a bruise everywhere

it remembers. I will ask you again
& again, *do you love me, do you
love me.*

Healing will be a heavy door.

                  II.

Your eyes will be sleepy
as almonds, I will eat from their view

until I am full with nurtured
perspective. You will roast

cumin seeds, while the fume hood sizzles,
drizzle my doubt into the granite mortar

of your mouth & pestle
it with your molars.

If your body were a star,
it would be cloves

& my pain would be dulled.
& if your body were a tambourine

your silver hair would jingle
when you laugh.

If your body were a picture,
I would find myself in it.

Healing will be a heavy door

& even if your body began in my head,
    you would be my backbone.

Thread and Tyre

Her motorcycle leather wilts halfway
off like a cocoon. Her skin, the crimped

fabric of a wing.
But she only fills me like thread
around a tyre.

Fast love, the leaning, the learning
without reading.

I was speechless, mostly because
I needed the letters aligned
with their facts,

but also, because I felt her lap my heart
again and again until its skin fell

the way you would from grace.
I was the miracle, my own maker,
but what good is a magic wand

in the hands of a rabbit.
I held my dreams like the day

they were born into and lured
myself back into a hat.

Am I real, or just not her.

Fast love, the grit on the road.
She was only a dream
on a spring day.

A face in the mirror
when neither of us was looking.

Acknowledgements

Thank you to the careful eyes, honest tongues and the brains, willing to run around in my poems. You true treasures, you know who you are.

Thank you Megan, for being my teacher. For pushing me past my limits to new adventures of writing. For creating such a loving, uplifting and supportive community with Poems That Don't Suck.

Thank you, my Love, for listening to me read my poetry to you after you've just had a long shift at work, after you've just woken up or while you're making dinner. Thank you for letting me cry more than I actually read. Thank you for being part of my process, in writing and in life.

My Father's Grief at the Kitchen Table was written after Warsan Shire's *The Unbearable Weight of Staying*.

Why I Hate March was written after *Why I Hate Raisins* by Natalie Diaz.

A Human Could Swim through a Whale's Veins was written after *The Nurse Lifts the Clipboard & Replaces all Your Vital Signs* by Noah Baldino / *Researchers Find The Father's DNA Stays in the Brains of Impregnated Women, Even Those Who Don't Carry to Term* by Meghann Plunkett.

To the Pigeons in the Underground Car Park was written after Hanif Abdurraqib's *For the Dogs Who Barked at Me on the Sidewalks of Connecticut*.

Nadine Klassen (she/her) is a German poet, living in her cozy hometown with her boyfriend and their dog. Her work focuses on mental health, trauma, relationships and identity. It has been published by Wild Roof Journal, Gnashing Teeth Publishing, Anti-Heroin Chic and others. She likes to write the occasional song on her guitar that's been missing a string for the better half of a year, practice drawing, or crochet sweaters with puffy sleeves. Bruises, Birthmarks & Other Calamities is her firstborn chapbook.

Also Available
from
Cathexis Northwest Press:

Something To Cry About
by Robert Krantz

Suburban Hermeneutics
by Ian Cappelli

God's Love Is Very Busy
by David Seung

that one time we were almost people
by Christian Czaniecki

Fever Dream/Take Heart
by Valyntina Grenier

The Book of Night & Waking
by Clif Mason

Dead Birds of New Zealand
by Christian Czaniecki

The Weathering of Igneous Rockforms in High-Altitude Riparian Environments
by John Belk

If A Fish
by George Burns

How to Draw a Blank
by Collin Van Son

En Route
by Jesse Wolfe

Sky Bright Psalms
by Temple Cone

Moonbird
by Henry G. Stanton

southern athiest, oh honey
by d. e. fulford

Cathexis Northwest Press